core belief™

Bible Study Series
for junior high/middle school

THE TRUTH ABOUT
Creation

Loveland, Colorado

The Truth About Creation

Core Belief Bible Study Series

Credits

Editors: Bob Buller, Lisa Baba Lauffer, and Helen Turnbull
Creative Development Editor: Michael D. Warden
Chief Creative Officer: Joani Schultz
Copy Editor: Debbie Gowensmith
Art Director: Bill Fisher
Computer Graphic Artist: Ray Tollison
Photographer: Craig DeMartino
Production Manager: Gingar Kunkel

Unless otherwise noted, Scriptures quoted from The Youth Bible, New Century Version, copyright © 1991 by Word Publishing, Dallas, Texas 75039. Used by permission.

ISBN 0-7644-0856-9

10 9 8 7 6 5 4 3 2 1   06 05 04 03 02 01 00 99 98 97

Printed in the United States of America.

core belief™

Bible Study Series
for junior high/middle school

contents:

the Core Belief: ▼Creation

Debates rage about how the world came into existence. Did God create it in six twenty-four-hour days? Did some kind of cosmic meeting of atoms explode into what we now call the universe? Your young people are in the middle of these debates, and they need answers.

God created everything that exists. Having no existing materials to work with, God created the universe by speaking it into existence, then forming this matter into an incredible variety of entities. His creation of the world was purposeful and has value. While everything God created was originally good, humanity sinned and brought suffering and death into God's creation. But God continues to have his guiding hand over his creation, and in the end—when he's completed his plan for evil and Satan—he'll create a new earth and a new heaven where there will be no more crying, pain, or death.

the ▼Helpful Stuff

▼Creation as a Core Christian Belief

The Bible begins with a simple declaration: "In the beginning God created the sky and the earth" (Genesis 1:1). That simple truth forms the foundation for all of Christian thought—about the world around us, the nature of humanity, even eternal life itself.

For example, the Bible teaches that every part of God's creation is good. Consequently, everything God created has value. Therefore, we shouldn't degrade, debase, or treat with contempt anything God has made—including ourselves and the world around us. Also, when God created us, he gave us responsibility and a purpose for living: God placed us on earth to represent him and to take care of his creation.

In the first study of *The Truth About Creation,* your kids will compare the different theories on the <u>creation</u> of the world to what the Bible says about creation. They'll discuss concerns they have with those theories and learn the indisputable truth that God created the universe.

Kids will continue their discussion on creation in the second study. They'll learn how they can care for the <u>environment</u> as servants of God and discover how they can be stewards of God's creation. Most importantly, they'll understand that because God wants them to care for the earth, their commitment to the environment is a commitment of faith.

The third study addresses kids' endless battle with <u>body image.</u> By helping kids understand that their true value comes from being created by God, they'll be able to see that they are God's masterpieces. By appreciating their physical worth as one of God's incredible accomplishments, kids can establish for themselves a high standard of self-respect.

The final study will help kids explore hard-to-answer questions in a lesson on <u>disease.</u> Kids who wonder how a loving God can exist when our world is filled with cancer, AIDS, heart disease, and other illnesses will realize how sin—not God—poisoned the world.

It's easy for young people today to lose sight of the important issues relating to creation. Too often they're distracted by the "battle" between creation and evolution or the various disagreements between Christians who interpret the biblical creation story differently. However, if your kids focus on the clear biblical teachings on creation, they can go into the world with a clear sense of who they are and where they fit within God's creation.

For a more comprehensive look at this Core Christian Belief, read Group's **Get Real: Making Core Christian Beliefs Relevant to Teenagers.**

DEPTHFINDER

HOW THE BIBLE DESCRIBES CREATION

To help you effectively guide your kids toward this Core Christian Belief, use these overviews as a launching point for a more in-depth study of creation.

● **God created all things that exist.** God, whose name means "I Am," is the only self-existing being. Everything else in the spiritual and physical worlds was created by God (Genesis 1:1; Isaiah 45:12; John 1:3; Ephesians 3:9; and Revelation 4:11).

● **God's first creative act brought the materials of the universe into existence.** God is eternal, but matter is not. God didn't use pre-existing materials to make the heavens and the earth. Rather, God created all that exists out of nothing simply by calling it into existence (Genesis 1:1; Mark 13:19; Romans 4:17; and Hebrews 11:3).

● **In later creative acts, God formed already existing matter into different entities.** After God called matter into existence, he shaped it into different objects and forms of life. For example, he created humans and animals out of the "dust of the ground" (Genesis 1:11-25; 2:4b-22; Job 33:6; Psalm 103:13-14; and 2 Peter 3:5).

● **God continues to preserve and guide creation.** God didn't set the world in motion and leave it to run on its own. God holds the universe together, maintains its existence, and guides it to accomplish his purposes (Nehemiah 9:6; Daniel 4:34-35; Matthew 6:26-30; 10:29; Colossians 1:17; and Hebrews 1:3).

● **Everything God created was originally good.** God designed and created the world so everything in it lived in complete harmony and perfect fulfillment of the purpose for which God created it. However, human sin polluted God's good creation and introduced death, disharmony, and destruction (Genesis 1:4, 10, 12, 18, 25, 31; 3:1-19; Proverbs 3:19-20; Romans 14:14-16; and 1 Timothy 4:4).

- **God created everything for a reason.** Nothing in God's creation is a product of chance. Everything has a purpose. For example, the planets and stars declare God's magnificence. As humans, we represent God on earth (Genesis 1:26-28; 2:18-24; 1 Chronicles 16:23-25; Psalm 19:1-4a; and Revelation 4:11).
- **Everything God created has value.** Since God created everything for some specific purpose, everything has value. Consequently, we shouldn't treat any part of creation with contempt. Rather we should treat everything with respect as God does (Job 38:41; Jonah 4:10-11; and Matthew 5:43-45; 6:26-30).
- **In the future, God will create a new heaven and earth.** Human sin corrupted God's creation, but God will accomplish his plan for creation. After God defeats Satan and sin and death, he will re-establish his creation in its original goodness and perfection (Isaiah 65:17-19; Romans 8:18-21; 1 Corinthians 15:20-28; Colossians 1:19-20; and Revelation 21:1–22:5).

CORE CHRISTIAN BELIEF OVERVIEW

Here are the twenty-four Core Christian Belief categories that form the backbone of Core Belief Bible Study Series:

The Nature of God	Jesus Christ	The Holy Spirit
Humanity	Evil	Suffering
Creation	The Spiritual Realm	The Bible
Salvation	Spiritual Growth	Personal Character
God's Justice	Sin & Forgiveness	The Last Days
Love	The Church	Worship
Authority	Prayer	Family
Service	Relationships	Sharing Faith

Look for Group's Core Belief Bible Study Series books in these other Core Christian Beliefs!

about

Bible Study Series
for junior high/middle school

Think for a moment about your young people. When your students walk out of your youth program after they graduate from junior high or high school, what do you want them to know? What foundation do you want them to have so they can make wise choices?

You probably want them to know the essentials of the Christian faith. You want them to base everything they do on the foundational truths of Christianity. Are you meeting this goal?

If you have any doubt that your kids will walk into adulthood knowing and living by the tenets of the Christian faith, then you've picked up the right book. All the books in Group's Core Belief Bible Study Series encourage young people to discover the essentials of Christianity and to put those essentials into practice. Let us explain...

What Is Group's Core Belief Bible Study Series?

Group's Core Belief Bible Study Series is a biblically in-depth study series for junior high and senior high teenagers. This Bible study series utilizes four defining commitments to create each study. These "plumb lines" provide structure and continuity for every activity, study, project, and discussion. They are:

● **A Commitment to Biblical Depth**—Core Belief Bible Study Series is founded on the belief that kids not only *can* understand the deeper truths of the Bible but also *want* to understand them. Therefore, the activities and studies in this series strive to explain the "why" behind every truth we explore. That way, kids learn principles, not just rules.

● **A Commitment to Relevance**—Most kids aren't interested in abstract theories or doctrines about the universe. They want to know how to live successfully right now, today, in the heat of problems they can't ignore. Because of this, each study connects a real-life need with biblical principles that speak directly to that need. This study series finally bridges the gap between Bible truths and the real-world issues kids face.

● **A Commitment to Variety**—Today's young people have been raised in a sound bite world. They demand variety. For that reason, no two meetings in this study series are shaped exactly the same.

● **A Commitment to Active and Interactive Learning**—Active learning is learning by doing. Interactive learning simply takes active learning a step further by having kids teach each other what they've learned. It's a process that helps kids internalize and remember their discoveries.

For a more detailed description of these concepts, see the section titled "Why Active and Interactive Learning Works With Teenagers" beginning on page 57.

So how can you accomplish all this in a set of four easy-to-lead Bible studies? By weaving together various "power" elements to produce a fun experience that leaves kids challenged and encouraged.

Turn the page to take a look at some of the power elements used in this series.

Betrayed!

HELPING KIDS DEAL WITH REJECTION FROM THE PEOPLE THEY LOVE

by Jennifer Carrell

THE POINT:

God is love.

■ Betrayal has very little shock value for this generation. It's as commonplace as compact discs and mosh pits. For many kids today, betrayal characterizes their parents' wedding vows. It's part of their curriculum at school; it defines the headlines and evening news. Betrayal is not only accepted—it's expected. ■ At the heart of such acceptance lies the belief that nothing is absolute. No vow, no law, no promise can be trusted. Relationships are betrayed at the earliest convenience. Repeatedly, kids see that something called "love" lasts just as long as it's ___ permanence. But deep inside, they hunger to see a

The Study AT A GLANCE

SECTION	MINUTES	WHAT STUDENTS WILL DO	SUPPLIES
Discussion Starter	up to 5	JUMP-START—Identify some of the most common themes in today's movies.	Newsprint, marker
Investigation of Betrayal	12 to 15	REALITY CHECK—Form groups to compare anonymous, real-life stories of betrayal with experiences in their own lives.	"Profiles of Betrayal" handouts (p. 20), highlighter pens, newsprint, marker, tape
	3 to 5	WHO BETRAYED WHOM?—Guess the identities of the people profiled in the handouts.	Paper, tape, pen
Investigation of True Love	15 to 18	SOURCE WORK—Study and discuss God's definition of perfect love.	Bibles, newsprint, marker
	5 to 7	LOVE MESSAGES—Create unique ways to send a "message of love" to the victims of betrayal they've been studying.	Newsprint, markers, tape
Personal Application	10 to 15	SYMBOLIC LOVE—Give a partner a personal symbol of perfect love.	Paper lunch sack, pens, scissors, paper, catalogs

notes:

● **A Relevant Topic**—More than ever before, kids live in the now. What matters to them and what attracts their hearts is what's happening in their world at this moment. For this reason, every Core Belief Bible Study focuses on a particular hot topic that kids care about.

● **A Core Christian Belief**—Group's Core Belief Bible Study Series organizes the wealth of Christian truth and experience into twenty-four Core Christian Belief categories. These twenty-four headings act as umbrellas for a collection of detailed beliefs that define Christianity and set it apart from the world and every other religion. Each book in this series features one Core Christian Belief with lessons suited for junior high or senior high students.

"But," you ask, "won't my kids be bored talking about all these spiritual beliefs?" No way! As a youth leader, you know the value of using hot topics to connect with young people. Ultimately teenagers talk about issues because they're searching for meaning in their lives. They want to find the one equation that will make sense of all the confusing events happening around them. Each Core Belief Bible Study answers that need by connecting a hot topic with a powerful Christian principle. Kids walk away from the study with something more solid than just the shifting ebb and flow of their own opinions. They walk away with a deeper understanding of their Christian faith.

● **The Point**—This simple statement is designed to be the intersection between the Core Christian Belief and the hot topic. Everything in the study ultimately focuses on The Point so that kids study it and allow it time to sink into their hearts.

● **The Study at a Glance**—A quick look at this chart will tell you what kids will do, how long it will take them to do it, and what supplies you'll need to get it done.

● The Bible Connection—This is the power base of each study. Whether it's just one verse or several chapters, The Bible Connection provides the vital link between kids' minds and their hearts. The content of each Core Belief Bible Study reflects the belief that the true power of God—the power to expose, heal, and change kids' lives—is contained in his Word.

THE POINT OF *BETRAYED!*:

God is love.

THE BIBLE CONNECTION

1 JOHN 4:7-21   The Apostle John explains the nature and definition of perfect love.

In this study, kids will compare the imperfect love defined in real-life stories of betrayal to God's definition of perfect love.

By making this comparison, kids can discover that God is love and therefore incapable of betraying them. Then they'll be able to recognize the incredible opportunity God off...

relationship worthy of their absolute trust.

Explore the verses in The Bible Connection...
mation in the Depthfinder boxes throughout...
understanding of how these Scriptures conne...

THE STUDY

DISCUSSION STARTER ▼

Jump-Start (up to 5 minutes) As kids arrive, ask them to thin... common themes in movies, books, TV show... have kids each contribute ideas for a mas... two other kids in the room and sharing... sider providing copies of People maga... what's currently showing on televisio... their suggestions, write their respons... come up with a lot of great ide... Even tho... ent, look through this list and... to discov... ments most of these themes... ave in comm...

After kids make several su...estions, mention... responses are connected w... the idea of betray...

● Why do you think... etrayal is such a co...

Betrayed! **17**

LEADER TIP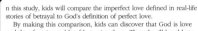

LEADER TIP for The Study
Because this topic can be so powerful and relevant to kids' lives, your group members may be tempted to get caught up in issues and lose sight of the deeper biblical principle found in The Point. Help your kids grasp The Point by guiding kids to focus on the biblical investigation and discussing how God's truth connects with reality in their lives.

DEPTHFINDER UNDERSTANDING INTEGRITY

Your students may not be entirely familiar with the meaning of integrity, especially as it might apply to God's character in the Trinity. Use these definitions (taken from Webster's II New Riverside Dictionary) and other information to help you guide kids toward a better understanding of how God maintains integrity through the three expressions of the Trinity.

Integrity: 1. Firm adherence to a code or standard of values. 2. The state of being unimpaired. 3. The quality or condition of being undivided.

Synonyms for integrity include probity, completeness, wholeness, soundness, and perfection.

Our word "integrity" comes from the Latin word *integritas*, which means soundness. *Integritas* is also the root of the word "integer," which means "whole or complete," as in a "whole" number.

The Hebrew word that's often translated "integrity" (for example, in Psalm 25:21 [NIV]) is *tam*. It means whole, perfect, sincere, and honest.

CREATIVE GOD-EXPLORATION ▼

Top Hats (18 to 20 minutes) Form three groups, with each trio member from the previous activity going to a different group. Give each group Bibles, paper, and pens, and assign each group a different hat God wears: Father, Son, or Holy Spirit...
...their goal is to write one list describing what God does in the... God's character.

● Depthfinder Boxes—These informative sidelights located throughout each study add insight into a particular passage, word, historical fact, or Christian doctrine. Depthfinder boxes also provide insight into teen culture, adolescent development, current events, and philosophy.

● Leader Tips—These handy information boxes coach you through the study, offering helpful suggestions on everything from altering activities for different-sized groups to streamlining discussions to using effective discipline techniques.

holy Profiles

Your assigned Bible passage describes how a particular person or group responded when confronted with God's holiness. Use the information in your passage to help your group discuss the questions below. Then use your flashlights to teach the other two groups what you discover.

■ Based on your passage, what does holiness look like?

■ What does holiness sound like?

■ When people see God's holiness, how does it affect them?

■ How is this response to God's holiness like humility?

■ Based on your passage, how would you describe humility?

■ Why is humility an appropriate human response to God's holiness?

■ Based on what you see in your passage, do you think you are a humble person? Why or why not?

■ What's one way you could develop humility in your life this week?

● Handouts—Most Core Belief Bible Studies include photocopiable handouts to use with your group. Handouts might take the form of a fun game, a lively discussion starter, or a challenging study page for kids to take home—anything to make your study more meaningful and effective.

The Last Word on Core Belief Bible Studies

Soon after you begin to use Group's Core Belief Bible Study Series, you'll see signs of real growth in your group members. Your kids will gain a deeper understanding of the Bible and of their own Christian faith. They'll see more clearly how a relationship with Jesus affects their daily lives. And they'll grow closer to God.

But that's not all. You'll also see kids grow closer to one another.

That's because this series is founded on the principle that Christian faith grows best in the context of relationship. Each study uses a variety of interactive pairs and small groups and always includes discussion questions that promote deeper relationships. The friendships kids will build through this study series will enable them to grow *together* toward a deeper relationship with God.

Big Bang? Big Botch?

EXPLORING CREATION AND EVOLUTION

THE POINT:

God created the universe.

■ How did we get here? The planet that we call home, the universe that our planet calls home—how were they created? Are we and our environment a huge accident, a result of compressed matter that happened to explode us all into existence? Or did a divine Creator intentionally and perfectly design earth to sustain life? ■ Most students get a one-sided view at school. The theory of evolution is taught as truth; the merest mention of the biblical creation story invites ridicule and is often forbidden. ■ Your kids need to hear the other side of the story. This study tells it to them.

by John Sanders

The Study
AT A GLANCE

SECTION	MINUTES	WHAT STUDENTS WILL DO	SUPPLIES
Creation Simulation	20 to 30	CREATE-A-WORLD—Create unique animals and an environment in which their creations can "survive."	Assorted craft materials as described in the "Before the Study" box (p. 17)
Bible Discovery	20 to 25	CREATION THEORIES—Compare various creation theories with the Bible's account of creation.	Bibles, "Creation Theories" handout (p. 22)
Closing	5 to 10	CREATION PRAYER—Read a responsive prayer proclaiming God as the creator of everything.	Animal creations from "Create-a-World" activity, "Creation Prayer" handouts (p. 23)

notes:

God created the universe.

THE BIBLE CONNECTION

GENESIS 1:1–2:3; NEHEMIAH 9:6; ISAIAH 45:5-7; AMOS 4:13; and COLOSSIANS 1:15-16

These passages proclaim God as the creator of the universe.

I n this study, kids will explore different theories about the creation of the world and will compare these theories to the Bible's account of creation.

Through this comparison, kids can discover God's role as creator of the universe.

Explore the verses in The Bible Connection; then examine the information in the Depthfinder boxes throughout the study to gain a deeper understanding of how these Scriptures connect with your young people.

BEFORE THE STUDY

For the "Create-a-World" activity, gather craft materials such as aluminum foil, modeling clay, construction paper, craft sticks, glue, tape, colored markers, newsprint, and other materials kids can use to create unique animals. The more materials you provide, the more creative your kids can be. Set these supplies in the middle of the room so everyone can have access to them.

For the "Creation Theories" activity, photocopy the "Creation Theories" handout (p. 22). Then cut apart the handout along the dotted lines. If you expect more than twenty students to participate in this study, make additional photocopies, and cut the handout into sections so every four students can have one creation theory.

For the "Creation Prayer" activity, make one photocopy of the "Creation Prayer" handout (p. 23) for each student.

LEADER TIP for The Study

Whenever you ask groups to discuss a list of questions, write the list on newsprint and tape it to a wall so groups can discuss the questions at their own pace.

THE STUDY

CREATION SIMULATION ▼

Create-a-World (20 to 30 minutes) When kids have arrived, say: **Today we'll explore how the universe was created. To start, let's do a little creating of our own. With the available supplies, each of you create an animal that has never been created. Do your best to create something entirely new. As you create your animal, think of what it needs to survive. For example, your animal may live in a lake of pudding or sleep on a nest of french fries.**

You have ten minutes to create. Have fun!

As kids work, walk around the room and compliment kids on their creativity and imagination. Invite kids to explain their animals to you. If some students seem stumped, suggest that they think of two or three of their favorite animals and somehow combine them to create original animals.

When kids have finished, have them work together to create an environment in your meeting room that will support all of their animals. For example, they could cut paper grocery bags into the shape of a lake to represent a lake of pudding. Or they could cover the walls with newsprint and draw landscapes on it.

When students are finished, have them sit in a circle. Have each student share with the rest of the class his or her animal creation, where it fits in the environment, and how it survives. If you have more than ten students, have kids form circles of four and explain the animals in their groups. Then have each young person say one way that the person on his or her right has been really creative, either in creating an animal, environment, or something outside of class. For example, "You were creative when you used foil to create a waterfall."

Then have kids form (or remain in) foursomes to discuss these questions:

● **How difficult was it for you to create your animal? for the class to create an environment where all the animals could exist? Explain.**

● **How difficult would it have been to create your animals and environment if I hadn't provided materials for you to use?**

● **How was the way you created your animals and environment like the way the world was created? How was it different?**

● **How do you think the universe came into existence?**

Then say: **If we were to interview people in this room about how we created this world and the animals in it, most would agree. But when it comes to explaining how the universe was created, people have conflicting views. Today we're going to explore a few theories of creation and evolution. As we do, think of whether you agree or disagree with this statement: <u>God created the universe.</u>**

DEPTHFINDER

UNDERSTANDING THESE KIDS

What do today's young people think about creation and evolution? Here are some opinions of young people who responded to religion and philosophy message boards for teenagers on America Online.

"When I first was reasoning out the idea of a God in my own mind, a thing that got me was that I knew of no alternative explanation for the creation of the world. I mean, I've heard of the Big Bang, etc., but that still starts with some matter already in the universe. Going back, doesn't there have to be a time when there was nothing? And how can you get something from nothing without God?"

—Brighte

"You can't say that God was always there and then say that the universe wasn't always there. If God can be there first, then anything else can be there first, too."

—Mist57

"Who says God didn't create the world as a soft, primitive thing, and then over the course of the "six days" (to him, at least; to us it is billions of years) he caused life to evolve? Maybe evolution is something that God created, and we're just figuring out?"

—TWIinfo

"The only reason behind the universe is because a bunch of particles of carbon and hydrogen bumped into each other."

—LaikaMF

"The God believer: God has no beginning, no end, and is eternal.
The atheist: The universe has no beginning, no end, and is eternal.
Who knows???"

—AmitaG

BIBLE DISCOVERY ▼

Creation Theories
(20 to 25 minutes)

Say: **Let's examine some explanations people give for the universe's creation.**

Have kids remain in their foursomes from the previous activity. Hand each foursome one of the sections of the "Creation Theories" handout, and have groups study their theories and the corresponding Scriptures. Then have groups develop creative ways to express what they learned from their studies. For example, the Big Bang theory group could hand out paper and challenge students to create something by wadding up their sheets of paper and throwing the wads against each other. Then the group could explain the Big Bang theory and explain how the corresponding Scripture passage supports or contradicts the theory.

When groups are ready, have them do their creative presentations. Invite kids to ask each other questions about their theories. If groups get stumped, help them answer the questions if you can.

Then have foursomes discuss these questions:

● **Which of the creation theories makes the most sense to you? Why?**

● **How was the way you expressed your theory like the way you were taught about the creation of the universe? How was it different?**

● **How do the Bible verses affect your beliefs about the universe's creation? Explain.**

When groups have finished their discussions, say: **We've examined a variety of the world's theories of creation. Now let's see what the Bible says about it.**

Assign one of the following passages to each of the theory groups. (If you had any groups exploring the same theories, have those groups gather together for this activity.)

- Big Bang Theory—Genesis 1:1-8
- Humanism—Genesis 1:9-13
- Spontaneous Generation—Genesis 1:14-19
- God created from existing matter—Genesis 1:20-23
- Pantheism—Genesis 1:24-31

Have groups read their passages, then find parts of the environment they created for their animals in the first activity that represent what their passages describe. For example, the first group could take a piece of their created environment that represents the sky.

After groups have chosen their items, say: **I'm going to read aloud the account of creation in the Bible. As I read the verses that your group is responsible for, bring your objects to the front of the room and do your best to form a picture of God's creation.** Read aloud Genesis 1:1–2:3, and have groups bring their objects to the front of the room and arrange them to convey how God created the universe. Ask:

● **How does the Bible's account of creation compare with the theories you studied earlier?**

● **How does the Bible's account of creation affect what you** believe about how the universe came into existence?

● **Could God have created the universe through some of the theories we studied today? Why or why not?**

Then have a volunteer read aloud Isaiah 45:18a: "The Lord created the heavens. He is the God who formed the earth and made it." Say: **People can argue all different theories, and some of those theories might explain part of the creation story. But the Bible tells the indisputable truth: that <u>God created the universe.</u>**

CLOSING ▼

Creation Prayer (5 to 10 minutes) Have kids gather their animal creations from the "Create-a-World" activity, form a circle, and place their creations in the middle of the circle. Then have students number off by twos.

Hand each student a copy of the "Creation Prayer" handout (p. 23), and say: **Today we've learned some different views of how the world was created. But the Bible, the Word of God, says that <u>God created the universe.</u>**

Let's thank God for his creation through a responsive reading. Look for your parts on the handout. The Ones will begin by reading the first line aloud together. Then the Twos will respond aloud together with their line. We'll proceed this way until we've read the whole prayer.

After the prayer, have kids gather their animals and take them home as reminders that <u>God created the universe.</u>

DEPTHFINDER UNDERSTANDING THE BIBLE

God at his very essence is the divine creator of the universe. Below are some additional Bible verses that express this truth. Make photocopies of this Depthfinder, and give one to each of your students so they can study the Scripture passages and discover more about the universe's creation.

● Isaiah 42:5—God created the skies and earth and gave life to humankind.

● Isaiah 64:8—God made all of us.

● Amos 5:8—God made the stars, morning, night, and the sea.

● Acts 4:24—God made the sky, the earth, the sea, and everything in them.

● 2 Peter 3:3-11—God continues to fulfill his plan for his creation.

● Revelation 21:1-5—In the end times, God will continue his creation by creating a new heaven and a new earth.

Creation Theories

BIG BANG THEORY

- This theory claims that matter (made up mostly of hydrogen and helium) compressed and then exploded to create the universe.
- Before the big explosion, all the matter and energy in the entire universe was squeezed together in a "cosmic egg," occupying very little (or no) space.
- After the "bang," single-celled organisms evolved into different multi-celled organisms, including humans.
- Scientists consider that the explosion continues to happen and our universe continues to expand.
  Bible reference: Genesis 1:1-2

HUMANISM

- This theory suggests that the universe is self-existing and not created.
- According to this theory, plants, animals, and humans were not created—they just came into existence by chance and natural processes.
- This theory also suggests that humans are part of nature and continually evolving.
  Bible reference: Colossians 1:15-16

SPONTANEOUS GENERATION

- This theory suggests that life (plants, animals, and humans) emerged from nonliving matter, meaning that life does not come from life.
- According to this theory, new creatures just appeared from nothing.
  Bible reference: Nehemiah 9:6

DUALISM

- This theory claims that God used previously existing matter to form the universe.
- God and matter both exist independent of a creator.
- God and matter are both eternal.
  Bible reference: Genesis 1:2 and Hebrews 11:3

PANTHEISM

- This theory suggests that many forces or gods contributed to the creation of the universe.
- These gods supposedly inhabit earthly things such as trees, rocks, and mountains.
- To some theorists, "God" is considered the process of evolution.
  Bible reference: Amos 4:13

Creation Prayer

The following responsive reading is adapted from Job 38:4-8, 11-12; and 39:26.

Ones: Where were you when God made the earth's foundations? Tell me, if you understand.

Twos: God created the universe. Who marked off how big the world should be? Who stretched a ruler across it?

Ones: God created the universe. What were the earth's foundations set on, or who put its cornerstone in place while the morning stars sang together and all the angels shouted with joy?

Twos: God created the universe. Who shut the doors to keep the sea in when it broke through and was born, when God said to the sea, "You may come this far, but no farther"?

Ones: God created the universe. Have you ever ordered the morning to begin or shown the dawn where its place was?

Twos: God created the universe. Is it through your wisdom that the hawk flies and spreads its wings toward the south?

Ones: God created the universe.

All: Thank you, God, for your creation.

Thinking Green

What Will It Take to Rescue the Earth?

THE POINT:

God wants you to take care of the earth.

■ Save the whales. Dolphin-free tuna. Biodiversity. Tread lightly on mother earth. These are catchy phrases for the nineties. But are they real concerns for youth today? A George H. Gallup International Institute survey shows that 90 percent of junior highers express concern about the environment (*America's Youth in the 1990s*). ■ Your kids know that caring for the environment is important to them. What they may not realize is that it's also important to God. Calvin B. DeWitt, director of the Au Sable Institute of Environmental Studies, a Christian center that integrates biblical studies and environmental science, acknowledges this lack of connection: "Today we often acknowledge God as Creator without grasping what it means to be part of creation…We abuse God's creation without realizing that we thereby grieve God" ("It's Not Biblical to be Green," Christianity Today, April 4, 1994). ■ Helping your young people understand what we as Christians can do to aid the environment will enable them to make a difference in today's environmental philosophies. This study will help teenagers understand how a commitment to the environment is a commitment of faith, and it will help kids define their roles as stewards for God's creation.

by Bill and Brooke Fisher

The Study
AT A GLANCE

SECTION	MINUTES	WHAT STUDENTS WILL DO	SUPPLIES
Active Opener	20 to 25	CLEAN IT UP—Make a documentary while collecting and disposing of litter from church grounds.	Trash bags, newsprint, marker, video camera and blank videotape or tape recorder and blank audiotape, "Story Assignment: Think Green" handout (p. 33)
Creative Participation	10 to 15	GLOBAL PASTING—Create globes from balloons and paste positive and negative environmental themes on them.	Large, uninflated, round balloons; glue; scissors; old magazines
Bible Exploration	5 to 10	WHAT'S GOD GOT TO SAY?—Explore God's Word to see what Scripture says about the environment and service.	Bibles, scrap paper, pens, video camera or tape recorder, tape from "Clean It Up" activity
Creative Closing	10 to 15	DEVOTION AND PRAYER—Reflect on creation and make a commitment as God's servants.	Key words in Scripture from "What's God Got to Say?" activity, video camera or tape recorder, TV and VCR or audiotape player, tape from "Clean It Up" activity, "Understanding the Environment" and "Understanding Community Outreach" Depthfinders (pp. 31 and 32)

notes:

God wants you to take care of the earth.

THE BIBLE CONNECTION

GENESIS 1:27-31	God creates humans in his image, instructs them to rule the world and everything in it, and gives plants and seeds to be food for all creatures.
HOSEA 4:1-3	God tells Israel that sins of the people are deteriorating the environment.
MATTHEW 20:25-28	Jesus calls Christians to be servants just as he is a servant.

I n this study, kids will examine God's creation and ways humanity has neglected it. Then kids will explore how to better serve God by acting as stewards of his creation.

Through this experience, kids can learn to model a positive attitude about God's creation and lead others in caring for the earth.

Explore the verses in The Bible Connection; then examine the information in the Depthfinder boxes throughout the study to gain a deeper understanding of how these Scriptures connect with your young people.

LEADER TIP for The Study

Whenever you ask groups to discuss a list of questions, write the list on newsprint and tape it to a wall so groups can discuss the questions at their own pace.

BEFORE THE STUDY

For the "Clean It Up" activity, gather one medium-sized trash bag for every two students. With a marker, write, "God wants you to take care of the earth" on a large sheet of newsprint; then place it outside on the church grounds where it can be easily spotted. Also, set up the video camera or tape recorder by making sure the batteries are charged and by loading and cueing a blank tape. Also make one photocopy of the "Story Assignment: Think Green" handout (p. 33).

You might want to prepare an opening for your documentary by reciting the title and credits at the beginning of the tape. For a video documentary, write the title and credits on a sheet of newsprint, and then film it.

For each student, photocopy the "Understanding the Environment" Depthfinder (p. 31) and the "Understanding Community Outreach" Depthfinder (p. 32).

LEADER TIP
for Clean It Up

Since your class will be outside, be sure to plan this activity for a fair-weather day. This activity would also work well as a field trip: Take kids to a nearby park, or volunteer your group with an adopt-a-highway program.

LEADER TIP
for Clean It Up

If you have an uneven number of students, stand in as videographer or sound person with one of the students. If you have more than ten students, use two or more video cameras or tape recorders.

LEADER TIP
for Clean It Up

If there's a breeze, place a rock on the newsprint with The Point written on it so the newsprint doesn't blow away.

THE STUDY

ACTIVE OPENER ▼

Clean It Up (20 to 25 minutes) Take the students outside, and divide them into pairs, giving one trash bag to each pair. Say: **Today we're going to study God's view of the environment. Let's start by walking around the church grounds and picking up trash. At the same time, we're going to make a documentary of our work.**

Have the pairs spread throughout the grounds to collect trash. Give the video camera or tape recorder to one pair. Designate this pair as the first video crew (or sound crew), and have the crew decide who will be the videographer (or sound person) and who will be the reporter. Give the reporter the "Story Assignment: Think Green" handout (p. 33) as instructions for interviews. Have the crew select another pair as subjects for the documentary. Tell the crew it has one minute of "A.T." (air time) to interview its subjects.

Tell the videographer to film the subjects as they collect trash and to shoot close-ups as the subjects respond to the reporter's questions. If you're using a tape recorder, have the sound person record the reporter's account of the setting and who he or she is about to interview.

When the crew is finished, have it stop the tape, hand off the camera or tape recorder and the "Story Assignment: Think Green" handout to the pair it interviewed and then designate that pair as the new video or sound crew. Have the new crew find another set of subjects to continue the documentary.

Have kids continue recording until each pair has acted both as the crew and as the subjects. Be sure to stop the tape after the last interview (and don't rewind the tape) so it's cued for later additions to your documentary.

After everyone has had a turn as a subject and on a crew, call the kids back together, meeting at the church's trash receptacle. Say: **While you were cleaning up the grounds, did anyone find a piece of newsprint with a message on it?**

Ask the student who found the piece of newsprint to read the message aloud. Then ask:

● **How have we just contributed to taking care of the earth?**

● **Why would <u>God want you to take care of the earth?</u>**

Have the kids place their trash in a trash receptacle or recycling bin. Save the newsprint with The Point written on it to use as a background for later videotaping. Say: **Now that we've helped clean up the church grounds, let's go back to the classroom to add to our documentary and discover more about how <u>God wants you to take care of the earth.</u>**

CREATIVE PARTICIPATION ▼

Global Pasting

(10 to 15 minutes)
Divide teenagers into groups of three or four. Designate a spot in the room for each group to gather. Hand each group a bottle of glue; some old magazines; scissors; and one large, uninflated, round balloon. Say: **Have someone in your group blow up the balloon.** When kids finish blowing up the balloons, say: **In your group, create an earth using the balloon as your model. Look through the magazines together, and cut out pictures or articles that convey how people have positively and negatively contributed to the earth's environment. Glue the positive and negative pictures and articles onto your earth. When everyone is done, each group will have one to two minutes to explain its earth to the class.** Allow each group five to seven minutes to create its earth.

Bring the groups back together, and ask a volunteer from each group to present its globe to the class. When all the groups finish presenting their globes, ask:

● **Did your group have a difficult time finding positive and negative examples in the magazines? Why or why not?**

● **Was there any positive or negative attributes on the globes that surprised you? Why or why not?**

● **Did you find more positive or more negative attributes in the magazines? Explain.**

● **Is your role in preserving the environment more positive or more negative? Explain.**

LEADER TIP
for Clean It Up

It's a good idea to move around with the crew so you can show kids how to use the video camera or tape recorder, help with mechanical problems, monitor the dialogue, and keep track of time.

DEPTH FINDER

UNDERSTANDING THESE KIDS

Teenagers are often portrayed as having a disinterest in the world and a low respect for authority. But according to *America's Youth in the 1990s* (George H. Gallup International Institute), this doesn't prove true with environmental issues.

● Ninety-three percent of teenagers agree with the statement, "Nature is God's creation and therefore it is the duty of humans to take care of the environment."

● Eighty-five percent of teenagers believe we should make laws requiring all citizens to conserve resources and reduce pollution.

● Forty-one percent of thirteen- to fifteen-year-olds are concerned a "great deal" about environmental problems.

● Twenty-seven percent of teenagers participated in 1992 in a group that protects the environment.

● Eighty-eight percent of teenagers voluntarily recycled newspapers, glass, aluminum, motor oil, or other items in 1992.

● Eighty percent of teenagers avoided using products that are harmful to the environment in 1992.

● Sixty-seven percent of thirteen- to fifteen-year-olds bought some product specifically because it was better for the environment than competing products.

● Sixty-four percent of thirteen- to fifteen-year-olds have tried to use less water.

LEADER TIP
for Global Pasting

Depending on the number of supplies, encourage the groups to share scissors and bottles of glue. If you prefer, use tape instead of glue to reduce messiness. Also encourage groups to trade magazines if they can't find what they're looking for. Have extra balloons on hand in case some balloons pop.

LEADER TIP

for Global Pasting

If you choose to use a video camera for the documentary you made in the "Clean It Up" activity, you may want to videotape your kids as they create and present their globes. Just be sure to leave plenty of space on the videotape to record the rest of the activities in the study.

● **How would your role change if you viewed caring for the environment as a means of serving God?**

● **Of all the positive attributes, which attributes most closely fit how <u>God wants you to take care of the earth</u>?**

Say: **Now that we've created the globes, we have a better understanding of the human effects on the earth. But what we may not understand is how our role in caring for the earth affects us. Let's document what God has to say about his creation and our role in it.**

BIBLE EXPLORATION ▼

What's God Got to Say? (5 to 10 minutes)

Lead the kids in a prayer thanking the Lord for his creation and inviting his wisdom during this Scripture study. Distribute Bibles, pens, and scrap paper. Have kids form pairs, and ask the kids in one of the pairs to act as the recorder and reader. Have the recorder use the video camera or tape recorder to record the reader as he or she reads the Scripture aloud to the rest of the group.

Have the kids look up Genesis 1:27-31. Ask the reader to recite the Scripture slowly, and have kids write down any key words or parts of the Scripture that are important to them. Then ask the following questions:

● **What are the key points of these verses in Genesis?**
● **What does this passage say about why God created plants?**
● **What are some reasons listed in this passage that <u>God wants you to take care of the earth</u>?**

Ask a different pair to act as the recorder and the reader. Have the recorder use the video camera or tape recorder to record the reader as he or she reads the Scripture aloud.

Have the kids look up Matthew 20:25-28 together. Ask the reader to recite the Scripture slowly, and have kids write down any key words or parts of the Scripture that are important to them. Then ask the following questions:

● **Why is it important to follow Jesus' example of servanthood?**
● **When we care for God's creation, are we servants? Why or why not?**
● **When we understand that <u>God wants us to take care of the earth,</u> who are we serving?**

Ask another pair to act as the recorder and the reader. Have the recorder use the video camera or tape recorder to record the reader as he or she reads the Scripture aloud.

Have kids look up Hosea 4:1-3 together. Ask the reader to recite the Scripture slowly, and have kids write down any key words or parts of the Scripture that are important to them. Then ask the following questions:

● **What did God have against Israel?**
● **Why was the land drying up and the animals and birds of the air dying?**
● **Do you think what happened to Israel could happen to the world today?**

● **How do these Scriptures impact your desire to take care of the earth?**

● **How will following Jesus help the environment and God's creation?**

Say: **God's Word holds powerful messages about the environment in which we live and about how <u>God wants you to take care of the earth.</u> As servants and followers of Jesus, we should always consider the authority that God has placed in our hands where his creation is concerned.**

Affirm the group by saying: **What we've seen in this study may leave you feeling overwhelmed. There's a lot to do as rulers over God's creation. But God never asks us to give more than we are able to. Each one of you has the ability to take care of the earth with God as your guide. Now let's close by asking for God's guidance.**

CREATIVE CLOSING ▼

Devotion and Prayer
(10 to 15 minutes)

Have the students remain in their pairs.
Say: **We know that <u>God wants you to take care of the earth,</u> and we've discovered different ways to do that. Now let's take some time to reflect on God's creation and our role as God's servants.** Rewind the videotape or audiotape, and play the documentary for the class. If you don't have time to review the entire tape, play a small segment from each activity you recorded. Then hand out one copy of the "Understanding the Environment" Depthfinder and the "Understanding Community Outreach" Depthfinder to each student.

Say: **With your partner, discuss the information on these**

DEPTHFINDER
UNDERSTANDING THE ENVIRONMENT

People often misunderstand the magnitude of throwing away recyclable items—or they may not realize what *is* recyclable. Following is a basic list of recyclable items:

Paper, glass, steel, plastics, newspapers, corrugated cardboard, glossy magazines and catalogs, office paper, aluminum scraps and cans, used carpet backing, and used motor oil. Recycling centers sometimes accept car batteries as well. Also, different recycling programs often accept paint and recycle it by mixing it with other paint remnants.

It may require some investigation to find places in your community that accept recyclable items. A good place to start is in your local phone book under "recycling services" or "garbage and rubbish collection." Also check with salvage yards or junk dealers to see if they pay for aluminum and other scrap metals.

handouts as well as the key words and important parts of Scripture from the last activity. **Choose one commitment you and your partner can make together as stewards of God's creation. Discuss how you'll help each other carry through with that commitment.**

Give teenagers two minutes to complete this task. When everyone has finished, have pairs take turns explaining their commitments to the rest of the class. Ask for volunteers to use the video camera or tape recorder to record the pairs' commitments as part of the class documentary. After each pair explains its commitment, have another pair comment on the positive effects of that commitment. Continue until every pair has explained its commitment and has made a positive comment.

Close with prayer, asking a volunteer to record the prayer as a closing for your documentary. Allow each teenager the chance to contribute. Say: **Lord, we've seen in this study that you want us to take care of the earth, and to you we give our service. We ask for your wisdom as we take care of the creation you have given us and as we fulfill the role you gave us in Scripture. May your blessings rest on each one of us as we commit to caring for your earth, and help us keep this commitment on a daily basis. In Jesus' name, amen.**

DEPTHFINDER UNDERSTANDING COMMUNITY OUTREACH

There are many ways to involve your youth group in making a positive impact in your community for the environment. Some of these also serve as great fund-raisers!

● Encourage teenagers to work together in setting up a church recycling program.

● Join a local highway-cleanup program.

● Collect aluminum cans throughout the community in a recycling drive. This can be a fund-raiser for your group if you take the cans to local recycling facilities for profit.

● Call a nearby wilderness agency, and have your youth group volunteer to help with the agency's labor tasks. Ask if their time may be traded for use of that agency's park facilities.

● Have your students start community awareness groups that network with schools, other youth groups, and local clubs.

Story Assignment: Think Green

Pick two questions from the list below, and ask one to each subject.

How much trash are you finding? Are you surprised by the litter you're collecting? Explain.

How do you feel about cleaning up the church's grounds?

Why do you think people litter?

Whose responsibility is it to clean up this litter?

Do you think it's worse to litter than to ignore litter? Why or why not?

What's the biggest environmental concern you have? Why?

How do you feel about humanity's role in preserving our environment? about your role?

On a scale of one to ten, how well do you take care of the earth?

Then ask both subjects the following question:

Do you think God wants you to care for the earth? Why or why not?

SUITABLE

FoR FRaMiNG

by Amy Simpson

Helping Youth Learn
to Value Their
Uniqueness

THE POINT:

You are God's masterpiece.

■ It's the latest epidemic. Junior highers are subjecting themselves to eating disorders, self-hatred, and expensive "remedies" for physical flaws. They buy magazines, the latest fashions, perfumes, colognes, and diet pills—all in the name of creating the right image. Society tells these teenagers that they should live up to an arbitrary and unrealistic standard of physical perfection, and many teenagers buy into this lie. In the process, however, they damage themselves and others. ■ Today's teenagers need to examine the standards upon which they are determining their physical worth. They also need to learn that our true value comes from being created by God. A study of God's creative power and the perfection of his creation can help teenagers see themselves as God sees them: as the pinnacle of his creation. ■ Understanding that each person is God's masterpiece is important to a study of creation because it highlights God's incredible accomplishments and our responsibility to accept ourselves as God created us. When we understand God's power and creative expertise, we can appreciate the way he created us. ■ This study provides an opportunity for teenagers to study God's creation, to examine the standards they hold for themselves, and to look at themselves as God sees them. As a result, they will be encouraged to look to God for their standards of value.

The Study
AT A GLANCE

SECTION	MINUTES	WHAT STUDENTS WILL DO	SUPPLIES
Opening	10 to 15	I SEE...—Make representations of themselves as they see themselves.	Paper, markers, scissors, magazines, pens or pencils, glue sticks, construction paper
Bible Study	20 to 25	A MASTER AT WORK—Study various aspects of God's creation and compare them to humanity.	Bibles, scissors, paper, pens or pencils, photocopies of "The Artist's Work" handout (pp. 43-44)
Critical Examination	10 to 15	PLAYING THE GAME—Play a game with unreasonable rules and compare these rules to the standards they use to view themselves.	Bibles, masking tape, newspaper, marker, newsprint
Closing	5 to 10	GOD SEES...—Re-create their representations of themselves based on how God sees them.	Paper, markers, scissors, trash can or recycling bin, magazines, pens or pencils, glue sticks, construction paper, small hand mirrors

notes:

You are God's masterpiece.

THE BIBLE CONNECTION

GENESIS 1:11-25	God creates plants, the sun and the moon, birds and water creatures, and land animals.
GENESIS 1:26-31	God creates humans and gives them their place in the world he has made.
PSALM 139:13-16	David describes God's personal and purposeful creation of him.
EPHESIANS 1:3-9	Paul talks about God's desire for each person he creates to know him.

I n this study, kids will compare their views of themselves with the way God sees them. They'll look at the quality and variety of God's creation and use what they learn to evaluate the standards they use to judge themselves and others.

By studying God's creation, kids can understand where real worth comes from and, as a result, learn to see themselves as God sees them.

Explore the verses in The Bible Connection; then examine the information in the Depthfinder boxes throughout the study to gain a deeper understanding of how these Scriptures connect with your young people.

BEFORE THE STUDY

Before the study, photocopy and cut apart the group assignments on "The Artist's Work" handout (pp. 43-44) for the "A Master at Work" activity. You'll need one copy of each section. If you have more than twenty teenagers, you may want to make one copy of the handout for every twenty kids.

For the "Playing the Game" activity, write the following questions on newsprint:

● **What do these verses say about God's creation of each person?**
● **What do these verses say about where our worth comes from?**
● **How should we respond to the way God created us and sees us?**

THE STUDY

OPENING ▼

I See... (10 to 15 minutes) As teenagers arrive, encourage each person to find his or her own space in the room. Give each person a sheet of paper. Set out markers, scissors, magazines, pens or pencils, glue sticks, and construction paper.

Say: **Use the materials I've provided to create a picture, sculpture, or other representation of how you see yourself physically. Be sure to include all the details. For example, if you think your nose is too big or your hair is too flat, include those details in the representation of yourself. Of course, be sure to include good features too. You won't have to show your self-representation to anyone else, so be honest. You'll have eight minutes to create your self-representation.**

After eight minutes, ask kids to think silently about their answers to the following questions. Pause for about thirty seconds after asking each question:

● **If you could change one thing about yourself, what would you change?**

● **Does your self-representation tend to focus on positive or on negative traits? Why?**

● **What standard do you use to determine what is or is not physically acceptable?**

● **How would you respond if I told you that <u>you are God's masterpiece?</u>**

Say: **Today we'll talk about who we think is beautiful, why we think those people are beautiful, and how this affects the way we see ourselves. We'll also discuss how God sees us and how this should affect the way we see ourselves. To get us started, let's take a look at the world God has created.** Have kids turn their self-representations face down and leave them in the space where they were working.

BIBLE STUDY ▼

A Master at Work (20 to 25 minutes) Have kids form four groups. Give each group several sheets of paper, pens or pencils, and one section of "The Artist's Work" handout (pp. 43-44).

Say: **Use the information on the handout to learn about one aspect of God's creation. Then think up a creative way to present the information on your handout to the other groups.**

DEPTH FINDER
UNDERSTANDING THESE KIDS

Eating disorders are an increasingly common result of the pressure kids feel to meet society's standards of physical beauty. According to TQ (Teen Quest) magazine, eating disorders affect nearly eight million Americans, including 11 percent of all high school seniors, 15 to 38 percent of college-age females, and 2 to 10 percent of college-age males (Julia McCarry, "Dying to Lose," March 1996).

The book *The Thin Disguise* lists the symptoms of two common eating disorders, anorexia nervosa and bulimia.

Common Symptoms of Anorexia Nervosa

1. The person thinks, *I'm much too fat*, even when emaciated.
2. The person voluntarily starves, which often leads to emaciation and sometimes death.
3. The person goes on occasional binges followed by fasting, laxative abuse, or self-induced starvation.
4. The person has an obsessive interest in recipes and cooking.
5. The person observes rituals involving food, exercise, and other aspects of life.
6. The person is perfectionistic.
7. The person has low self-esteem.
8. The person exercises excessively.
9. The person is introverted and withdrawn; he or she avoids people.
10. The person maintains rigid control.
11. The person is characterized by depression, irritability, deceitfulness, guilt, and self-loathing.
12. [In a woman, her] period stops.

Common Symptoms of Bulimia

1. The person is caught up in the binge-purge syndrome.
2. The person is usually within ten to fifteen pounds of ideal body weight.
3. The person is a secretive binge eater. Binges may occur regularly and may follow a pattern. Caloric intake per binge may range from 1,000 to 20,000 calories.
4. The person binges; these are followed by fasting, laxative abuse, self-induced vomiting, or other forms of purging. The person may chew food but spit it out before swallowing.
5. The person may often experience fluctuations in weight because of alternating periods of bingeing and fasting.
6. The person observes rituals involving food, exercise, and other aspects of life.
7. The person is perfectionistic.
8. The person wants relationships and approval of others.
9. The person loses control and fears being unable to stop once he or she begins eating.

For more information on anorexia nervosa and bulimia, *The Thin Disguise* is an excellent resource (Pam Vredevelt, et al., Thomas Nelson Publishers, 1992).

LEADER TIP

for A Master at Work

If you have more than twenty students in your group, you may want to form eight groups and have two groups make presentations on each section of the handout.

You can perform a skit or a pantomime, write a song, tell a story with actions involving the other groups, give a speech that uses visual aids, or do something else. Your presentation should last less than five minutes. The only rule is that everyone in your group must be involved in your presentation. You'll have ten minutes to prepare your presentation.

After ten minutes, call kids back together and, starting with group 1, have each group make its presentation. Lead kids in enthusiastic applause after each presentation.

When groups have finished their presentations, ask the entire group:

● **What did these presentations teach you about God? about the things he created?**

● **What do these amazing facts tell us about the way God made each part of his creation?**

Say: **Your presentations have shown us some great examples of God's creative power and artistic variety. And God was definitely happy with what he made. You probably noticed that at the end of each day, God said his creation was good. But it got even better. Let's take a look at the very last thing God created.**

Read Genesis 1:26-31 aloud. Ask:

● **What's the difference between humanity and the rest of creation?**

● **What's the relationship between humanity and the rest of creation?**

● **What does the story of God's creation teach us about how God sees us?**

Say: **God created us with incredible variety, intelligence, and value. He sees us as valuable and proclaimed us as *very* good. In other words, <u>you are God's masterpiece.</u>**

Unfortunately, we often focus on things we don't like about ourselves. So let's play a game to discover why we often feel as though we don't measure up.

CRITICAL EXAMINATION ▼

LEADER TIP

for Playing the Game

When kids discuss a list of questions within small groups, write the list on newsprint and tape it to a wall so groups can discuss the questions at their own pace.

Playing the Game (10 to 15 minutes)

Use masking tape to place a line down the middle of the room. Have kids form two teams. Instruct teams to line up, facing each other, with one team on each side of the tape line. Then have one person on each team stand three to five feet behind the rest of the team and hold his or her arms in front to form a circle. Instruct each "goal person" to stand in one place during the entire game. Give each team a stack of newspapers that have been separated into individual pages.

Say: **The object of this game is for your team to be the first to get your entire stack of newspaper through the arms of the goal person on the other team. You can put only one page through at a time. You can cross the center line to do this, but you cannot touch members of the other team at any time. Finally, you also want to keep the other team from getting its newspaper through** the arms of your goal person. **Go!** If kids ask for more information, simply repeat the rules you already gave them.

While kids play the game, stop the action every thirty to sixty seconds to present new rules that give an unfair advantage to one team. Introduce the following rules to only one team, one rule at a time:

- **You cannot cross the middle line.**
- **You must sit down and stay seated.**
- **You may not crumple the newspaper.**
- **You may not reach your arms into the air.**
- **You are not allowed to throw newspaper.**

When all the rules have been introduced or when one team has won the game, call the end of the game. Ask the entire group:

- **How did you feel about the rules I introduced into the game? How did the rules affect the way you played?**
- **How are these rules like the rules we use to decide who's good-looking? How are they different?**
- **Who makes the rules about physical looks? Why do you think people are so eager to follow these rules?**
- **Who do you think has the right to determine who is good-looking? who has worth?**
- **What things determine your worth? What things really don't affect your true worth?**

Say: **People today often base their worth on how good others think they look, but God doesn't play that game. The story of creation teaches us that God created humans just as he wanted them. But what about every person as an individual? Are all people equally valuable? Let's take a look at the way God sees each person.**

Have kids stay in their teams from the game. Tape to a wall the newsprint with questions that you prepared before the study. Assign each team either Psalm 139:13-16 or Ephesians 1:3-9. Have each team read its Scripture passage and then discuss the questions on the newsprint.

After five minutes, ask for volunteers to read the Scripture passages to the entire group. Then have each team report its answers to the questions. Say: **Because you are God's masterpiece, God wants you to see yourself as he sees you: as his special creation. And when you see yourself as God's masterpiece, you'll be able to accept yourself just as God created you.**

"You made my whole being;
you formed me in my mother's
body. I praise you because
you made me in an amazing
and wonderful way. What you
have done is wonderful. (I)
know this very well."

—Psalm 139:13-14

DEPTHFINDER
UNDERSTANDING THESE KIDS

If you recognize the symptoms of an eating disorder in one of your group members, it's probably best to approach his or her parents with your concerns. Then you and the parents can work together to help your group member face and overcome the eating disorder. *The Thin Disguise* (Pam Vredevelt, et al.) offers the following guidelines for parents of a child with an eating disorder:

- Lovingly confront an anorexic or bulimic with his or her symptoms.
- Get professional help for family members under legal age.
- Get support for yourself.
- Learn about eating disorders.
- Require the anorexic or bulimic to take responsibility for his or her actions.
- Recognize any lies you have come to believe about the anorexic's or bulimic's behavior.
- Talk openly and honestly about your feelings.
- Be honest with an anorexic or a bulimic about his or her appearance.
- Talk about issues other than food.
- Listen.
- Show love and affection.
- Hang in there!

CLOSING ▼

God Sees... (5 to 10 minutes) Have students go back to the space where they left their self-representations in the "I See…" activity. When everyone is settled, pray aloud, asking God to help your kids see themselves from God's perspective instead of in relation to the arbitrary standards set up by society.

Give each person a sheet of paper. Set out markers, scissors, magazines, pens or pencils, glue sticks, and construction paper.

Take around a trash can or recycling bin to each person, and say to the group: **You're going to make new representations of yourselves, so let's throw the old ones away. Use the materials I've provided to create a new representation of yourself, this time based on how God sees you. Basically, you'll be creating your own masterpiece to reflect God's valuable creation—you.**

When kids finish creating their self-representations, have them form pairs. Then have partners answer the following questions:

- **How is this self-representation different from your first one? How is it the same?**
- **What can you do to see yourself as God sees you? to accept yourself as God made you?**

Then go to each person, and give him or her a small hand mirror. As you hand each person a mirror, say: **You are God's masterpiece.** Have kids take their mirrors and new self-representations home as reminders of their worth as God's creations.

The Artist's Work

Group 1

Read Genesis 1:11-13.

Using this Scripture passage, the amazing facts below, and any other information you'd like, create a presentation to teach the other groups about God's creation. Be sure to focus on what these amazing facts teach us about God's creative power and design.

Amazing Facts About Plants

● Forests of sea kelp plants stretch from the ocean floor to the water's surface, providing food, homes, and safe hiding places for all kinds of sea creatures (Ranger Rick, January 1996).

● Forest fires actually rejuvenate old forests. Ashes provide minerals for new plants to feed on. The heat of the fire also causes pine cones full of seeds to pop open and spread their seeds. Finally, new plants receive more sunlight for growth after tall trees are destroyed (Ranger Rick, October 1995).

● Peanuts grow down, not up. A bee pollinates a flower on a peanut vine, the flower dries up and falls off, and the vine grows down into the ground. Once it's underground, the tip of the vine grows into a pod, inside of which grow peanuts (Ranger Rick, February 1995).

● Plant seeds find all kinds of ways to travel and form new plants. Many seeds are carried by the wind. Others are shot into the air when the pods they grow in dry out and shrink, squeezing the seeds out. Some plants grow fruit full of seeds. The fruit attracts animals, who eat the fruit and spread the seeds in their feces. Other seeds grow in waterproof shells that float and wash up on faraway beaches. Finally, some prickly seeds get free rides on humans or on animals who brush up against them (Ranger Rick, November 1994).

● Plants use energy provided by the sun to make their own food. The sun's energy causes water and carbon dioxide inside the leaves to mix and then feed the plant (Ranger Rick, June 1994).

 • • • • (cut here) •

Group 2

Read Genesis 1:14-19.

Using this Scripture passage, the amazing facts below, and any other information you'd like, create a presentation to teach the other groups about God's creation. Be sure to focus on what these amazing facts teach us about God's creative power and design.

Amazing Facts About the Sun and the Moon
(from Ranger Rick, June 1994)

● The sun is made of about seventy different gases, all combined in the right proportions to warm and sustain life on our planet. The sun is about 93 percent hydrogen, about 6 percent helium, and about 1 percent other gases.

● The sun doesn't burn like fire does. The heat and light created by the sun come from a much more intricate process. The hydrogen atoms in the sun crash together to make helium. This nuclear reaction in the sun creates energy, which is released in the form of heat and light.

● Moons are unique stellar bodies, much different from the way we usually think of them. The moon doesn't shine; it doesn't create its own light. Instead, it reflects the light of the sun shining on it. The sun, therefore, actually provides light for us twenty-four hours a day.

● The sun is hotter than anything on earth. The temperature of the sun is about 27 million degrees Fahrenheit in the middle and about 10,300 degrees Fahrenheit on the surface. The temperature of the sun and the distance between the sun and the earth are perfect for allowing life to thrive on earth. If the sun were closer, we would burn up; if it were farther away, we would freeze.

● Compared to other stars, the sun is only medium-sized. It is about 865,000 miles wide, though. If the sun were the size of a basketball, the earth would be the size of a pinhead. Other stars are much larger, but they appear smaller because they're farther away from the earth.

The Artist's Work

Group 3

Read Genesis 1:20-23.

Using this Scripture passage, the amazing facts below, and any other information you'd like, create a presentation to teach the other groups about God's creation. Be sure to focus on what these amazing facts teach us about God's creative power and design.

Amazing Facts About Birds and Water Creatures

● Squids have tiny sacs of color on their skin. Squids can change the size of these sacs, which alters their color or creates a different color pattern. They do this to signal other squids, to threaten enemies, or to disguise themselves to match their surroundings (Ranger Rick, December 1993).

● When it's time for birds to mate, male birds use various techniques to win female birds. Male birds show off their flying abilities, snuggle with the females, bring them food or nest-building materials, make themselves look attractive, make attractive sounds, build impressive homes, strut around, or whistle (Ranger Rick, March 1995).

● Alligator snapper turtles blend in with their surroundings on the bottoms of rivers. They have small pieces of pink flesh on the bottom of their mouths that look like worms. The turtles sit still with their mouths open. Fish who see the pink things waving in the water go after the "worms," and then the turtles eat the fish (Ranger Rick, October 1995).

● Owls can't move their eyes from side to side, but they can turn their heads all the way to the backs of their bodies. Some burrowing owls line their homes with cow droppings to keep their enemies from smelling the owls inside. When their enemies do go into owls' homes, burrowing owls make a sound like that of a rattlesnake, which scares the enemies away (Ranger Rick, April 1993).

● Trumpetfish, sailfish, sawfish, and paddlefish have extremely long snouts for various reasons. Trumpetfish use their snouts to "vacuum up" other fish. The sawfish uses the sharp edges of its snout to snag fish to eat. Sailfish use their snouts like swords, slashing through schools of fish and eating the dead or injured prey. The paddlefish's snout is covered with sensors that help it find food. It has no teeth, but its mouth is the size of a one-gallon jug of milk. It swims with its mouth open, catching food in its path (Ranger Rick, March 1995).

••• (cut here) ••

Group 4

Read Genesis 1:24-25.

Using this Scripture passage, the amazing facts below, and any other information you'd like, create a presentation to teach the other groups about God's creation. Be sure to focus on what these amazing facts teach us about God's creative power and design.

Amazing Facts About Land Animals

● Camels can go for more than two weeks without drinking. When they do drink, they can guzzle twenty-seven gallons of water in ten minutes (Ranger Rick, October 1995).

● Some snakes can go for more than a year without eating, but a shrew may starve to death in six hours (Ranger Rick, October 1995).

● In snowy climates, many animals—such as the snowshoe hare and the lynx—have large feet that help them run quickly across the snow without sinking (Ranger Rick, December 1993).

● Elephants use their trunks for various purposes, including breathing while they're underwater, greeting other elephants, playing, fighting, squirting water into their mouths, spraying themselves, picking leaves, and throwing rocks. Elephants can even be trained to haul heavy loads or to paint pictures (Ranger Rick, August 1996)!

● Komodo dragons—the world's biggest lizards—have germs in their saliva that can cause deadly infections. If they bite an animal and the animal gets away, the animal will probably die in a day or two. Then the Komodo dragon can sniff out the odor of the dead animal and eat it (Ranger Rick, October 1993).

● Many animals have features that alter their appearance and enable them to drive their enemies away. The man-faced bug looks as though it has a large face on its back, making it look like a much larger creature. Some caterpillars can make themselves look like snakes. Finally, some South American frogs with fake eyes on their back ends can blow themselves up with air until they look like strange and scary creatures (Ranger Rick, October 1995).

OUTBREAK!

Helping Young People **UNDERSTAND**
the Physical and Spiritual Effects of the **FALL**

by Lisa Baba Lauffer

■ When was the last time you heard of someone dying from "natural causes"? It seems that diagnosis has almost completely disappeared from our culture. Even those who die when elderly often experience complicating circumstances: cancer, heart disease, multiple sclerosis, leukemia, and other diseases. And people often point to the existence of disease when claiming that a loving God couldn't possibly exist. "If there's an all-powerful and all-loving God somewhere out there, how could he allow people to suffer?" The questions become more impassioned when they hit close to home: "How could God allow my best friend to suffer?" "Why did God give my mom cancer?" or "Why do I have diabetes?" ■ Your kids need to discover the true source of disease in our world: sin. Instead of pointing to God as the one who allowed sin's entrance into our world, they need to look at sin's impact not only on our spiritual well-being, but also on our physical well-being. In this study, your young people will do just that.

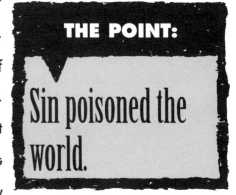

THE POINT:

Sin poisoned the world.

The Study
AT A GLANCE

SECTION	MINUTES	WHAT STUDENTS WILL DO	SUPPLIES
Introduction	10 to 15	DIAGNOSIS: ?—Choose cards indicating whether they've contracted a "disease."	Bibles, "Health Cards" handouts (p. 55), scissors, red-dot stickers, paper, marker, tape
Bible Exploration	15 to 20	SIN DOES A BODY BAD—Brainstorm about the effects of disease, list the effects of sin as described in several Bible passages, and compare and contrast the two categories.	Bibles, newsprint, marker, masking tape, self-stick notes, blue pens, black pens, "Health Cards" handouts (p. 55), red-dot stickers
Object Lesson	10 to 15	ONE FOR ALL—Do an activity based on one person's choice and then discuss how, through one person, we're all sinful.	Bibles; "One for All" handout (p. 56); scissors; hat, box, basket, or paper bag; red-dot stickers
Response	10 to 15	ONE DIED FOR ALL—Write prayers to God in response to the rest of the study and attach their written prayers to a cross using their red-dot stickers.	Bibles, slips of paper, pens, masking tape

notes:

Sin poisoned the world.

THE BIBLE CONNECTION

GENESIS 2:16-17 and 3:6-19, 23-24	Adam and Eve disobey God's command to avoid eating from the tree of knowledge, and God outlines the consequences of their disobedience.
EZRA 9:6; PROVERBS 29:6; ISAIAH 59:2; JEREMIAH 5:25; EZEKIEL 16:52; and TITUS 3:3	These passages describe various effects of sin.
ROMANS 5:12-14	Paul explains how sin causes death.
ROMANS 5:15-19	Paul rejoices that Christ's death pays for the sins of all humanity.

I n this study, kids will experience an outbreak of an imaginary disease, resulting in each person contracting the "disease" by the end of the study. Along the way, kids will do activities and object lessons illustrating how sin affects us all physically and spiritually.

Through these experiences, kids can realize that Adam and Eve's original sin introduced the realities of disease to the world. Your students can also realize that, while they can't escape the consequences of sin on this earth, they can entrust their lives to Jesus Christ and so experience eternal life free from disease and sin.

Explore the verses in The Bible Connection; then examine the information in the Depthfinder boxes throughout the study to gain a deeper understanding of how these Scriptures connect with your young people.

LEADER TIP for The Study

Because this topic can be so powerful and relevant to kids' lives, your group members may be tempted to get caught up in issues and lose sight of the deeper biblical principle found in The Point. Help your kids grasp The Point by guiding them to focus on the biblical investigation and by discussing how God's truth connects with reality in their lives.

BEFORE THE STUDY

Make enough copies of the "Health Cards" handout (p. 55) so each student can have one copy of the "Diagnosis: Positive" card and one copy of the "Clean Bill of Health" card. Cut apart and fold each card. Then arrange the cards into two piles, placing an equal number of "Diagnosis: Positive" cards and "Clean Bill of Health" cards into each pile.

Make one photocopy of the "One for All" handout (p. 56), and cut apart the tasks. Fold each slip of paper, and place the slips into a hat, box, basket, or paper bag.

Draw an outline of a person on a large piece of newsprint. Tape the newsprint to one wall of your meeting room.

INTRODUCTION ▼

Diagnosis: ? (10 to 15 minutes) After everyone has arrived, use a marker to write "Quarantined" on piece of paper; then tape the paper to the outside of the classroom door. Gather students together, and say: **Before we all came into this room, an extremely sick person was in here.**

This person has a deadly and highly contagious disease. The disease travels in airborne cells. As a result of just coming into this room, we've all been exposed; more than likely, each of us will contract the disease.

Throughout today's study, we'll take "card tests" to determine whether we've caught the disease. I'll hand you a card, and the card will indicate whether you've been "infected." The card I hand you will either say, "Diagnosis: Positive," which means you have the disease, or it'll say, "Clean Bill of Health," which means you don't...yet. If you receive a "Diagnosis: Positive" card, indicate so by taking one of the red-dot stickers and placing it over your heart. Place all of the red-dot stickers in a central location for students to obtain during the study. (You can buy red-dot stickers at your local office-supplies store.)

Have each student turn to a partner to discuss these questions:

● **What's your initial reaction to the news that you could contract a disease? that this possibility is a result of someone else's presence in this room?**

● **Do you have any experience with a real disease, such as having one yourself or knowing someone who has one? If so, what was your experience, and what was your reaction to it?**

● **What do you think and feel about living in a world where you and those you love can get diseases?**

When pairs have finished their discussions, say: **It's time for our first card test.** Give each student one of the folded slips from one of the piles you prepared before the study, and instruct kids to look at their cards. Have each student who receives a "Diagnosis: Positive" card take a red-dot sticker and place it over his or her heart. Then have students return to their partners to discuss these questions:

● **How do you feel now that you've been diagnosed with or without the disease?**

● **How might the way you feel right now be like the way someone feels when a doctor gives him or her a positive or negative diagnosis?**

● **How would your partner be a good friend to someone who has a serious illness? For example, your partner might be a faithful friend who would keep a sick person company.**

DEPTHFINDER UNDERSTANDING THE BIBLE

While exploring this study's topic, some of your students may turn a skeptical eye toward God. "Why," they may ask, "would a loving God put the tree of knowledge in the garden, knowing that humankind would mess up, eat the fruit, and reap the deathly consequences?"

Why *couldn't* God just put man and woman in the Garden of Eden and allow them to live in bliss without the possibility of temptation? In the *Teacher's Commentary,* Lawrence O. Richards sheds some light on this issue: "This opportunity to eat was no trap, or even a test. Given the intention of God that man should be in His own image, that tree was a necessity! There is no moral dimension to the existence of a robot; it can only respond to the program imposed by its maker. Robots have no capacity to value, no ability to choose between good and bad, or good and better. To be truly like God, man must have the freedom to make moral choices and the opportunity to choose, however great the risk such freedom may involve."

God lovingly made the choice to give us choice, wanting to give us ultimate freedom. And while humankind didn't remain faithful to God, he remained faithful to us, providing us yet another chance to choose life by sending Jesus Christ to die in our place.

Have each pair find another pair, and have the newly formed foursomes read Genesis 2:16-17 and 3:6-19. Then have foursomes discuss these questions:

● **What did God command Adam and Eve? How did Adam and Eve respond to this command?**

● **What consequences did God set down because of Adam and Eve's disobedience?**

● **How might these consequences contribute to the fact that we have disease in our world?**

● **How is our scenario of one sick person possibly infecting all of us in this room like Adam and Eve's disobedience making us all vulnerable to the effects of sin, including disease? How is it different?**

● **What's your reaction to facing consequences because Adam and Eve sinned?**

When foursomes have finished their discussions, invite students to share their responses with the whole class. Then say:  **<u>Sin poisoned the world.</u> When Adam and Eve chose to disobey God's command against eating from the tree of knowledge, they set in motion consequences that all of humankind experiences. You can see it in the decaying of our world, especially when diseases weaken those we love or even ourselves. We're going to explore this a little further during today's study.**

LEADER TIP for Diagnosis: ?

Because the story of the Fall can be a difficult concept for kids to understand, be sure to read the two "Understanding the Bible" Depthfinders to prepare yourself for kids' questions.

DEPTHFINDER UNDERSTANDING THE BIBLE

Adam and Eve's sin didn't affect humankind alone. According to Romans 8:20-22, "Everything God made was changed to become useless, not by its own wish but because God wanted it and because all along there was this hope: that everything God made would be set free from ruin to have the freedom and glory that belong to God's children. We know that everything God made has been waiting until now in pain, like a woman ready to give birth." The *Disciple's Study Bible* further elaborates: "Three statements underlie the eager expectation of creation: because of human sin, God subjected the created order to frustration...; the created order is presently in bondage to decay; and it has been and yet continues to groan with birth pains. The analogy of travail suggests the coming to be of something new. Creation is not what it should be due to human sin. It cannot serve its true function of glorifying God. It decays and thus goes nowhere. It is temporary rather than eternal. It suffers pain rather than being the arena of peace."

This sounds so hopeless, but God promises a new earth one day (Revelation 21:1-5) and redeemed bodies for those who choose to entrust their lives to him (Romans 8:23). Though things often seem bleak, we have this promise to cling to: "The sufferings we have now are nothing compared to the great glory that will be shown to us" (Romans 8:18). When your students feel discouraged by the disease of those they love and the decay of the earth, encourage them to remember that God has in store something perfect and unblemished, something far greater in beauty and purity than they could ever imagine.

BIBLE EXPLORATION ▼

Sin Does a Body Bad

(15 to 20 minutes) With the class still together, ask kids to brainstorm about diseases they've heard of such as cancer, the ebola virus, AIDS, leukemia, multiple sclerosis, diabetes, and heart disease. Then say: **Now I'm going to have you return to your foursomes to brainstorm about the effects of disease in general. Think not only of physical effects, but of emotional, relational, and spiritual effects. For example, one emotional effect of disease can be the feeling of isolation. As you brainstorm, tap into your own experiences. If you've had a disease or known someone who has a disease, think about the effects you've observed or experienced.**

Before you begin, assign a role to each person in your group. Assign one person in your group to be the recorder. This person will write each idea on a separate self-stick note. Also assign one person to be presenter 1, who will share your answers with the whole class; assign another to be the encourager, who will make sure each person has an opportunity to speak; and assign another person to be presenter 2, who will present information to the class later in this activity.

Hand each group a stack of self-stick notes and a blue pen. Allow groups about two minutes to brainstorm. Then invite each group's presenter 1 to share effects the group came up with and attach each corresponding self-stick note to an appropriate place on the person outline you prepared before the study. For example, if a group included the effect of "feeling isolated," the presenter could place that self-stick note over the outline person's heart.

After all groups have presented, ask:

● **What's your reaction to seeing all these effects of disease?**

● **What do you think it's like for a person to endure some or all of these effects of disease?**

Once you've finished the discussion, have students return to their foursomes. Assign each foursome one or two of the following passages (if you have more than seven foursomes, give the same passage to more than one group): Genesis 3:14-19, 23-24; Ezra 9:6; Proverbs 29:6; Isaiah 59:2; Jeremiah 5:25; Ezekiel 16:52; and Titus 3:3. Also hand each foursome a black pen. Say: **Read the passages I've assigned to your group. As you do, look for the effects of sin as described in your passage. On a separate self-stick note, write each effect you read. This is important: Use your black pen to write these effects. This will help us distinguish between the effects of disease and the effects of sin. Presenter 2 will share your ideas with the rest of the class.**

Allow groups two minutes to read their passages and write their ideas. Then have each foursome's presenter 2 state each effect his or her group discovered in the Bible passage and place the corresponding self-stick note on an appropriate place on the person outline. For example, if one group writes, "Sin separates us from God," it could place the corresponding self-stick note outside the person outline.

When all the groups have presented their findings, ask the whole class:

● **According to your findings, how are the effects of disease similar to the effects of sin? How are they different?**

● **Could some of the effects of sin cause some of the effects of disease? If so, how?**

● **Does this activity illustrate the idea that <u>sin poisoned the world</u> and specifically our bodies? Why or why not?**

Say: **Let's be clear about one thing. <u>Sin poisoned the world</u> in a *general* sense. In no way do we want to turn from this activity or today's study, point to people with diseases, and say to them, "You have a disease because you've sinned." In some cases, that might be true, but it's not up to us to say one way or the other. We *are* saying that Adam and Eve's *original* sin exposed us all to the effects of sin, one of which is disease. We *all* have susceptibility to disease because we live in a sinful world. To signify this, we're going to take another card test.**

To all the students who do not yet have a red-dot sticker, pass out one slip of paper from the second pile of diagnosis cards. Have kids open their diagnosis cards at the same time. Then have kids who received "Diagnosis: Positive" cards place red-dot stickers over their hearts.

Ask:

● **How do you feel about your diagnosis?**

● **How do you feel right now as you see even more of you "falling" to our disease?**

● **How is this like seeing more people fall to the effects of sin such as disease? How is it different?**

LEADER TIP for Sin Does a Body Bad

Groups may have a difficult time figuring out the effects of sin from their Bible passages. As groups do this part of the activity, circulate throughout the room, and help any groups that seem stumped.

LEADER TIP

for The Study

More than likely, you'll have one or two students who either have diseases themselves or are close to someone who has a disease. These students can be excellent sources of information for this topic; allow these students to share from their experiences if they wish. Also remain sensitive to these students' feelings. They may need to process feelings about their diseases or the diseases of those they love.

Be careful not to communicate to these students that they (or their loved ones) have contracted a disease because *they sinned*. You don't want to add that extra, and extraneous, burden to your students. If kids seem confused about this, clarify that disease came into the world because of original sin and that most individuals don't contract diseases because of sin in their own lives. You could encourage these students to read John 9:1-3, the story about people accusing a blind man or his parents of having sinned, therefore causing his blindness. Have students pay particular attention to Jesus' response in verse 3.

Say: **We can tangibly see the effects of sin's destruction in those who suffer from diseases. In the next activity, we'll discover that because <u>sin poisoned the world</u>, we all experience sin's effects in some way.**

OBJECT LESSON ▼

One for All (10 to 15 minutes)

Choose a volunteer from the class. Hold out the container with the slips of paper cut from the "One for All" handout (p. 56), and have the volunteer choose one slip and read aloud what it says. For a few seconds, allow the student to think he or she must do the task by himself or herself. Then say: **What our volunteer has chosen, everyone in this room must do.** Read aloud the slip the volunteer has chosen, and tell students to follow the instruction.

After everyone has done the task, have students return to their foursomes and discuss these questions:

● **What's your reaction to having to do something that someone else chose for you?**

● **Have you ever been in other situations in which someone else's choices or behavior affected you? If so, what were those situations, and how did you feel?**

● **Have you ever done something that has affected someone else? If so, what and how did you feel?**

Then have foursomes read Romans 5:12-14 and discuss these questions:

● **What does this passage say about the way sin came into the world?**

DEPTH FINDER — UNDERSTANDING DISEASE

In *Two-Part Invention: The Story of a Marriage*, author Madeleine L'Engle shares her struggles of watching her husband lose a long, strenuous, and painful battle with cancer. As she recounts her experiences, L'Engle expresses her thoughts about sin's effect on the world: "We human beings have free will, and disease is a result of our abuse of that free will throughout the centuries." She elaborates further: "My friend Tallis remarked once that cancer is the result of sin, not the sin of the person suffering from this ugly disease, but the sins of many human beings throughout the ages, making wrong choices, letting greed override wisdom.

"This abuse of free will throughout the millennia does not mean that cancer is a punishment, as some people view it. No, it is a consequence of many actions by many people, often unknowing."

Your students may struggle with The Point of this study, thinking that disease is a punishment from God and fretting over loved ones who've fallen prey to cancer, heart disease, or other illnesses. If your students wrestle with such thoughts, read them L'Engle's perspective, ask your students about their perspectives, and pray with them that God will make *his* perspective clear to them.

● What does this passage say are the consequences of Adam's sin? Who suffers these consequences?

● How is having to do the task our volunteer chose like experiencing sin because of Adam's choice? How is it different?

● How do you feel knowing that one person's actions have impacted your life, causing you to suffer the consequences of sin?

● Does this passage explain the existence of disease in the world? If so, how?

Say: <u>**Sin poisoned the world.**</u> **When Adam and Eve chose to eat the forbidden fruit, the whole world paid the price. You and I have been affected as has the rest of God's creation. To symbolize this, those of you who have not yet been declared ill now no longer have a clean bill of health. Each of you must take a red-dot sticker to signify that you've experienced the disease.**

Allow kids time to place stickers on their shirts.

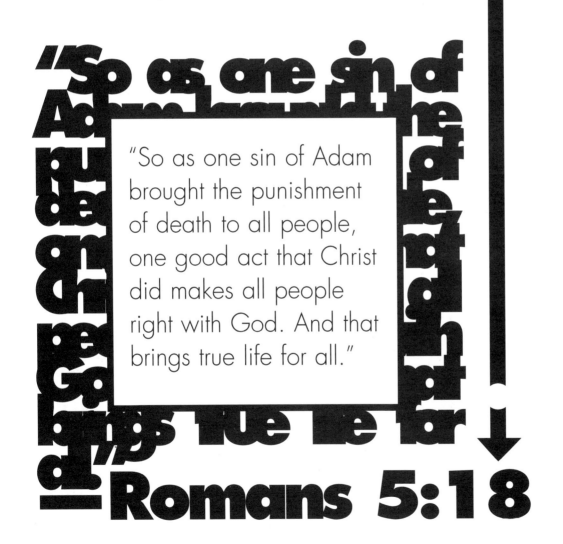

"So as one sin of Adam brought the punishment of death to all people, one good act that Christ did makes all people right with God. And that brings true life for all."

—Romans 5:18

One Died for All

(10 to 15 minutes) Say: **We've discussed a very bleak topic today. It's not easy to express how disease affects people, especially if we've had any kind of exposure to it in our own lives. But the story doesn't end there. While we can't completely eradicate disease from the earth—though many compassionate people spend their lives researching cures—we can eradicate spiritual disease and death from our lives for eternity.**

Have students return to their foursomes to read Romans 5:15-21 and discuss these questions:

● **How does Christ's action counteract the consequences of Adam's sin?**

● **What were the spiritual results of Christ's action?**

After foursomes discuss the passage, invite students to share their insights with the whole class. Then give each student a slip of paper and a pen. Have each student find a spot away from other students for some introspective time. Then say: **As you spend time alone, consider how you'd like to respond to what you read in Romans 5:15-21. You might want to reread the passage. Then, if you wish, write a prayer to God. You can write a prayer thanking him for sending Jesus to die so that we could all have life. You could write a prayer telling him that while you don't feel ready to give your life to him, you want to discover more about him. Or maybe you want to write a prayer asking God to heal a family member, friend, or yourself from a disease.**

As students spend time alone, use masking tape to create an outline of a cross on one wall of your meeting room (see diagram in the margin).

After about three minutes, encourage students to finish writing their prayers. When most students seem done, say: **We all have stickers over our hearts symbolizing that we've all been touched by the effects of Adam and Eve's sin. For some of us, that means we experience disease in our lives, whether in ourselves or in others. For some of us, we experience sin's consequences in other ways. But God has made a way for all of us to be free of those consequences for eternity. If we give our lives to Jesus Christ, who died for the sins of the world, he will cleanse us of all our sin, allowing us to experience eternal life. While we'll still experience the effects of living in a sinful world, we can celebrate the truth that someday we will be in heaven with Jesus, in a place where there will be no more disease or sickness. To symbolize this, I'd like each of us to fold our slips of paper, remove our stickers, and attach our folded slips of paper to this cross using our stickers. This doesn't mean that you've made a commitment to Christ; it will illustrate, though, that we all have the opportunity to receive God's free gift of grace.**

Before dismissing students, say a quick prayer of thanks that through one man—Jesus Christ—we all can be free from the result of one original sin.

Health Cards

Before the study, make enough copies of this handout so each student can have one copy of the "Diagnosis: Positive" card and one copy of the "Clean Bill of Health" card. Cut apart and fold each card. Then arrange the cards into two piles, placing an equal number of "Diagnosis: Positive" cards and "Clean Bill of Health" cards into each pile.

DIAGNOSIS: POSITIVE	**CLEAN BILL OF HEALTH**
DIAGNOSIS: POSITIVE	**CLEAN BILL OF HEALTH**
DIAGNOSIS: POSITIVE	**CLEAN BILL OF HEALTH**
DIAGNOSIS: POSITIVE	**CLEAN BILL OF HEALTH**

ONE FOR ALL

Make one photocopy of this handout, and cut apart the tasks. Fold each slip of paper, and place the slips into a hat, box, basket, or paper bag.

··· ✂ (cut here)

Show how you'd react if you were on your deathbed.

··· ✂ (cut here)

Show how you'd react if a doctor just told you that you have cancer.

··· ✂ (cut here)

Show how you'd react if you were in a hospital and needed a nurse's immediate attention.

··· ✂ (cut here)

Show how you'd react if a friend or family member just told you he or she has a terminal illness.

why ▼ Active and Interactive Learning works with teenagers

Let's Start With the Big Picture

Think back to a major life lesson you've learned.

Got it? Now answer these questions:

● Did you learn your lesson from something you read?

● Did you learn it from something you heard?

● Did you learn it from something you experienced?

If you're like 99 percent of your peers, you answered "yes" only to the third question—you learned your life lesson from something you experienced.

This simple test illustrates the most convincing reason for using active and interactive learning with young people: People learn best through experience. Or to put it even more simply, people learn by doing.

Learning by doing is what active learning is all about. No more sitting quietly in chairs and listening to a speaker expound theories about God—that's passive learning. Active learning gets kids out of their chairs and into the experience of life. With active learning, kids get to *do* what they're studying. They *feel* the effects of the principles you teach. They *learn* by experiencing truth firsthand.

Active learning works because it recognizes three basic learning needs and uses them in concert to enable young people to make discoveries on their own and to find practical life applications for the truths they believe.

So what are these three basic learning needs?

1. Teenagers need action.

2. Teenagers need to think.

3. Teenagers need to talk.

Read on to find out exactly how these needs will be met by using the active and interactive learning techniques in Group's Core Belief Bible Study Series in your youth group.

1. Teenagers Need Action

Aircraft pilots know well the difference between passive and active learning. Their passive learning comes through listening to flight instructors and reading flight-instruction books. Their active learning comes through actually flying an airplane or flight simulator. Books and lectures may be helpful, but pilots really learn to fly by manipulating a plane's controls themselves.

We can help young people learn in a similar way. Though we may engage students passively in some reading and listening to teachers, their understanding and application of God's Word will really take off through simulated and real-life experiences.

Forms of active learning include simulation games; role-plays; service projects; experiments; research projects; group pantomimes; mock trials; construction projects; purposeful games; field trips; and, of course, the most powerful form of active learning—real-life experiences.

We can more fully explain active learning by exploring four of its characteristics:

● **Active learning is an adventure.** Passive learning is almost always predictable. Students sit passively while the teacher or speaker follows a planned outline or script.

In active learning, kids may learn lessons the teacher never envisioned. Because the leader trusts students to help create the learning experience, learners may venture into unforeseen discoveries. And often the teacher learns as much as the students.

● **Active learning is fun and captivating.** What are we communicating when we say, "OK, the fun's over—time to talk about God"? What's the hidden message? That joy is separate from God? And that learning is separate from joy?

What a shame.

Active learning is not joyless. One seventh-grader we interviewed clearly remembered her best Sunday school lesson: "Jesus was the light, and we went into a dark room and shut off the lights. We had a candle, and we learned that Jesus is the light and the dark can't shut off the light." That's active learning. Deena enjoyed the lesson. She had fun. And she learned.

Active learning intrigues people. Whether they find a foot-washing experience captivating or maybe a bit uncomfortable, they learn. And they learn on a level deeper than any work sheet or teacher's lecture could ever reach.

● **Active learning involves everyone.** Here the difference between passive and active learning becomes abundantly clear. It's like the difference between watching a football game on television and actually playing in the game.

The "trust walk" provides a good example of involving everyone in active learning. Half of the group members put on blindfolds; the other half serve as guides. The "blind" people trust the guides to lead them through the building or outdoors. The guides prevent the blind people from falling down stairs or tripping over rocks. Everyone needs to participate to learn the inherent lessons of trust, faith, doubt, fear, confidence, and servanthood. Passive spectators of this experience would learn little, but participants learn a great deal.

● **Active learning is focused through debriefing.** Activity simply for activity's sake doesn't usually result in good learning. Debriefing—evaluating an experience by discussing it in pairs or small groups—helps focus the experience and draw out its meaning. Debriefing helps sort and order the information students gather during the experience. It helps learners relate the recently experienced activity to their lives.

The process of debriefing is best started immediately after an experience. We use a three-step process in debriefing: reflection, interpretation, and application.

Reflection—This first step asks the students, "How did you feel?" Active-learning experiences typically evoke an emotional reaction, so it's appropriate to begin debriefing at that level.

Some people ask, "What do feelings have to do with education?" Feelings have everything to do with education. Think back again to that time in your life when you learned a big lesson. In all likelihood, strong feelings accompanied that lesson. Our emotions tend to cement things into our memories.

When you're debriefing, use open-ended questions to probe feelings. Avoid questions that can be answered with a "yes" or "no." Let your learners know that there are no wrong answers to these "feeling" questions. Everyone's feelings are valid.

Interpretation—The next step in the debriefing process asks, "What does this mean to you? How is this experience like or unlike some other aspect of your life?" Now you're asking people to identify a message or principle from the experience.

You want your learners to discover the message for themselves. So instead of telling students your answers, take the time to ask questions that encourage self-discovery. Use Scripture and discussion in pairs or small groups to explore how the actions and effects of the activity might translate to their lives.

Alert! Some of your people may interpret wonderful messages that you never intended. That's not failure! That's the Holy Spirit at work. God allows us to catch different glimpses of his kingdom even when we all look through the same glass.

Application—The final debriefing step asks, "What will you do about it?" This step moves learning into action. Your young people have shared a common experience. They've discovered a principle. Now they must create something new with what they've just experienced and interpreted. They must integrate the message into their lives.

The application stage of debriefing calls for a decision. Ask your students how they'll change, how they'll grow, what they'll do as a result of your time together.

2. Teenagers Need to Think

Today's students have been trained not to think. They aren't dumber than previous generations. We've simply conditioned them not to use their heads.

You see, we've trained our kids to respond with the simplistic answers they think the teacher wants to hear. Fill-in-the-blank student workbooks and teachers who ask dead-end questions such as "What's the capital of Delaware?" have produced kids and adults who have learned not to think.

And it doesn't just happen in junior high or high school. Our children are schooled very early not to think. Teachers attempt to help kids read with nonsensical fill-in-the-blank drills, word scrambles, and missing-letter puzzles.

Helping teenagers think requires a paradigm shift in how we teach. We need to plan for and set aside time for higher-order thinking and be willing to reduce our time spent on lower-order parroting. Group's Core Belief Bible Study Series is designed to help you do just that.

Thinking classrooms look quite different from traditional classrooms. In most church environments, the teacher does most of the talking and hopes that knowledge will transmit from his or her brain to the students'. In thinking settings, the teacher coaches students to ponder, wonder, imagine, and problem-solve.

3. Teenagers Need to Talk

Everyone knows that the person who learns the most in any class is the teacher. Explaining a concept to someone else is usually more helpful to the explainer than to the listener. So why not let the students do more teaching? That's one of the chief benefits of letting kids do the talking. This process is called interactive learning.

What is interactive learning? Interactive learning occurs when students discuss and work cooperatively in pairs or small groups.

Interactive learning encourages learners to work together. It honors the fact that students can learn from one another, not just from the teacher. Students work together in pairs or small groups to accomplish shared goals. They build together, discuss together, and present together. They teach each other and learn from one another. Success as a group is celebrated. Positive interdependence promotes individual and group learning.

Interactive learning not only helps people learn but also helps learners feel better about themselves and get along better with others. It accomplishes these things more effectively than the independent or competitive methods.

Here's a selection of interactive learning techniques that are used in Group's Core Belief Bible Study Series. With any of these models, leaders may assign students to specific partners or small groups. This will maximize cooperation and learning by preventing all the "rowdies" from linking up. And it will allow for new friendships to form outside of established cliques.

Following any period of partner or small-group work, the leader may reconvene the entire class for large-group processing. During this time the teacher may ask for reports or discoveries from individuals or teams. This technique builds in accountability for the teacherless pairs and small groups.

Pair-Share—With this technique each student turns to a partner and responds to a question or problem from the teacher or leader. Every learner responds. There are no passive observers. The teacher may then ask people to share their partners' responses.

Study Partners—Most curricula and most teachers call for Scripture passages to be read to the whole class by one person. One reads; the others doze.

Why not relinquish some teacher control and let partners read and react with each other? They'll all be involved—and will learn more.

Learning Groups—Students work together in small groups to create a model, design artwork, or study a passage or story; then they discuss what they learned through the experience. Each person in the learning group may be assigned a specific role. Here are some examples:

Reader

Recorder (makes notes of key thoughts expressed during the reading or discussion)

Checker (makes sure everyone understands and agrees with answers arrived at by the group)

Encourager (urges silent members to share their thoughts)

When everyone has a specific responsibility, knows what it is, and contributes to a small group, much is accomplished and much is learned.

Summary Partners—One student reads a paragraph, then the partner summarizes the paragraph or interprets its meaning. Partners alternate roles with each paragraph.

The paraphrasing technique also works well in discussions. Anyone who wishes to share a thought must first paraphrase what the previous person said. This sharpens listening skills and demonstrates the power of feedback communication.

Jigsaw—Each person in a small group examines a different concept, Scripture, or part of an issue. Then each teaches the others in the group. Thus, all members teach, and all must learn the others' discoveries. This technique is called a jigsaw because individuals are responsible to their group for different pieces of the puzzle.

JIGSAW EXAMPLE

Here's an example of a jigsaw.

Assign four-person teams. Have teammates each number off from one to four. Have all the Ones go to one corner of the room, all the Twos to another corner, and so on.

Tell team members they're responsible for learning information in their numbered corners and then for teaching their team members when they return to their original teams.

Give the following assignments to various groups:

Ones: Read Psalm 22. Discuss and list the prophecies made about Jesus.

Twos: Read Isaiah 52:13–53:12. Discuss and list the prophecies made about Jesus.

Threes: Read Matthew 27:1-32. Discuss and list the things that happened to Jesus.

Fours: Read Matthew 27:33-66. Discuss and list the things that happened to Jesus.

After the corner groups meet and discuss, instruct all learners to return to their original teams and report what they've learned. Then have each team determine which prophecies about Jesus were fulfilled in the passages from Matthew.

Call on various individuals in each team to report one or two prophecies that were fulfilled.

You Can Do It Too!

All this information may sound revolutionary to you, but it's really not. God has been using active and interactive learning to teach his people for generations. Just look at Abraham and Isaac, Jacob and Esau, Moses and the Israelites, Ruth and Boaz. And then there's Jesus, who used active learning all the time!

Group's Core Belief Bible Study Series makes it easy for you to use active and interactive learning with your group. The active and interactive elements are automatically built in! Just follow the outlines, and watch as your kids grow through experience and positive interaction with others.

FOR DEEPER STUDY

For more information on incorporating active and interactive learning into your work with teenagers, check out these resources:

● *Why Nobody Learns Much of Anything at Church: And How to Fix It,* by Thom and Joani Schultz (Group Publishing) and
● *Do It! Active Learning in Youth Ministry,* by Thom and Joani Schultz (Group Publishing).

your evaluation of

Bible Study Series
for junior high/middle school

the truth about
CREATION

Group Publishing, Inc.
Attention: Core Belief Talk-Back
P.O. Box 481
Loveland, CO 80539
Fax: (970) 669-1994

Please help us continue to provide innovative and useful resources for ministry. After you've led the studies in this volume, take a moment to fill out this evaluation; then mail or fax it to us at the address above. Thanks!

● ● ● ● ● ●

1. As a whole, this book has been (circle one)

not very helpful   very helpful
1   2   3   4   5   6   7   8   9   10

2. The best things about this book:

3. How this book could be improved:

4. What I will change because of this book:

5. Would you be interested in field-testing future Core Belief Bible Studies and giving us your feedback? If so, please complete the information below:

Name _____

Street address _____

City _____ State _____ Zip _____

Daytime telephone (____) _____ Date _____

THANKS!